TECUMSEH
Shawnee War Chief

by Jane Fleischer
illustrated by Hal Frenck

Troll Associates

Troll Associates, Mahwah, N.J.

Library of Congress Catalog Card Number: 78-18046
ISBN 0-89375-153-7

TECUMSEH

Shawnee War Chief

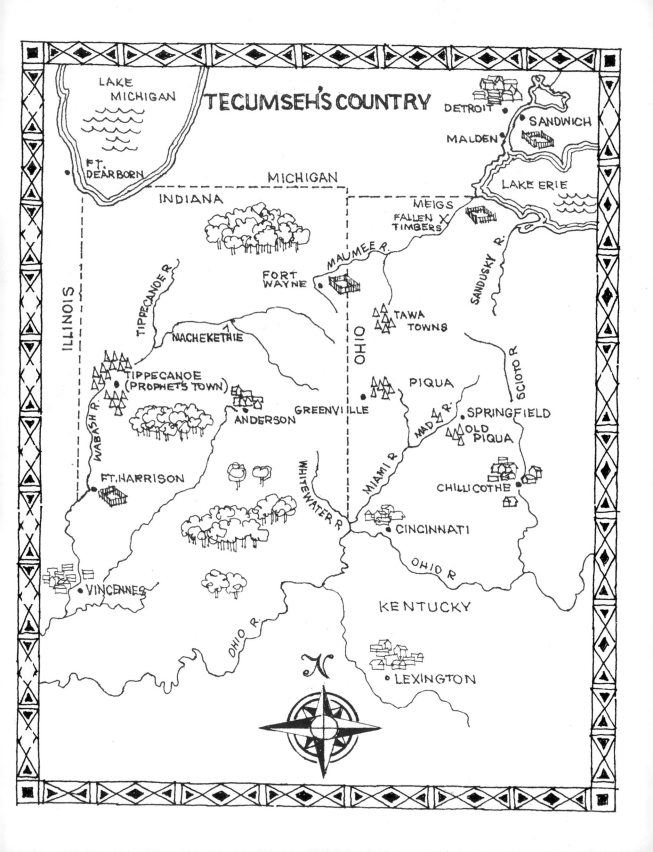

Tecumseh sat up suddenly. Once again, he had been awakened by the war drums. He knew that his father and the other men of the village would be preparing for battle.

The young boy had lived most of his life under the clouds of war. He was born in the small village of Old Piqua, on the banks of the Mad River in Ohio. His father was Puckeshinwa, a Shawnee Chief.

The Shawnee Nation was the largest group of tribes in Ohio. They built large villages and planted acres of corn. They hunted on the vast, rich lands of the Ohio Valley.

For many years, Puckeshinwa had welcomed the traders who bought the Shawnees' furs. French and English traders had always moved freely on the winding rivers. The Shawnees wished only to live in peace on their land.

But the peace in Ohio had ended. Now smoke signals carried the news of war from one Shawnee village to the next.

Settlers in western Virginia were claiming that Shawnee land belonged to them. Their leader, Lord Dunmore, led a strong army to take the Shawnee land.

Tecumseh was too young to understand, but he watched proudly as Puckeshinwa told the warriors of his village that they must go into battle.

But the Indians' bows and arrows were no match for the soldiers' guns. Soon, the Shawnees had lost most of their hunting grounds south of the Ohio River. Tecumseh's father was killed in the fighting.

All his life, Tecumseh would remember his mother's grief when she heard of his father's death.

Now Cheeseekau, his oldest brother, became Tecumseh's teacher. He taught the boy all the skills of a woodsman, hunter, and warrior. Tecumseh learned well.

In their village, the boys played war games. Tecumseh was always a leader.

10

Sitting at the campfire, young Tecumseh listened with pride to the old stories of his people. Although the Shawnees had no books, their long history was told again and again.

Each winter, Tecumseh took time to mend the wigwams of the old and the poor. When he returned from hunting, he brought back meat for those who could not hunt for themselves.

Cheeseekau was proud of his young brother.

With each season, the Shawnees' troubles with the settlers grew worse. After the American War for Independence, a steady stream of settlers began to pour into the rich farmlands of Kentucky and Ohio.

When he was only fifteen, Tecumseh rode with war parties to attack and burn the flatboats coming up the river.

As the frontier wars raged, Tecumseh saw his own village burn!

His mother had now seen enough of war. She took his small brother and sisters to find a safe home. Tecumseh was to travel with his brother Cheeseekau.

For the last time, Tecumseh looked at the ashes of his village. He had lost his father and an older brother in the fighting with the settlers. Now he had lost his home, and his family was being scattered. The fires of hate burned in his heart!

All the way from Florida to the Great Lakes, Indians were being forced to move from their hunting grounds. It was a time of great change and unhappiness.

By 1786, most of the Shawnee people had moved into northeastern Ohio and eastern Indiana. But Cheeseekau, Tecumseh, and many other young warriors stayed to defend their land.

When word came that the Cherokees in Tennessee needed help, Cheeseekau's band of warriors rode south. But this was the last time Tecumseh would fight at his brother's side.

Cheeseekau was killed in battle, and Tecumseh vowed to take many lives for this loss. Although he was the youngest member of the group, he was a brave fighter. The warriors made him their Chief.

Soon, they were fighting settlers and soldiers in Georgia, Florida, Alabama, and Mississippi.

After several years, Tecumseh returned to the
North. Smoke signals carried word of more war
through the Ohio Valley. Never before had so
many soldiers marched against the Indians.

The Shawnees fought bravely, but they were
outnumbered. One Indian village after another
was burned to the ground. Fields of corn were
destroyed. Hunting grounds were ruined. Hunger
and sadness broke the spirit of many tribes.

16

In the spring of 1795, at Greenville, Ohio, the Chiefs of twelve tribes signed a peace treaty. They agreed to give up huge areas of rich land to the Americans.

Tecumseh refused to meet with them. How could a few Chiefs give away land that belonged to all Indians? He would sign nothing!

17

Instead, Tecumseh moved just west of the treaty line, on the banks of the Wabash River. Many warriors followed him.

Tecumseh did not believe the settlers would stay on their own side of the line. Only time would tell.

He was troubled as he saw the sorrow of his homeless people. Not only the Shawnees, but all the tribes in the North and South were being pressed west toward the setting sun.

In his heart, Tecumseh believed there was only one way to save the Indian way of life. If he could unite the tribes from the Gulf of Mexico to the Great Lakes, they would have great strength.

United, the Indians would be able to keep the settlers from destroying what was left of their land.

Tecumseh began to speak of this dream of one Indian Nation. Soon, he had followers from many tribes.

Tecumseh's younger brother, Tenskwatawa, now joined him. Tenskwatawa, too, dreamed of peace for the Indians. He believed the Great

Spirit had given him magic powers. He said he could tell the future. They called him the Shawnee Prophet.

The Prophet gave hope to the homeless Indians who followed him. He promised that through his magic power, all white men would be destroyed. He said that all the great warriors who had been killed in battle would live again, and that the wild game would return to the hunting grounds.

Tecumseh did not believe in such magic. But his brother taught people to turn from the ways of the white man and to take up the old customs of Indian life. Tecumseh believed in this with all his heart.

In time, Tecumseh and Tenskwatawa built a large village, called Tippecanoe, on the banks of the Wabash River.

As the seasons passed, Tecumseh spent more and more time away from Tippecanoe. He found followers among the young Chiefs of the Delaware, Ottawa, Ojibwa, Wyandot, and Kickapoo tribes.

William Henry Harrison, governor of the Indiana Territory, kept a close watch on the trails that led to and from Tippecanoe. He did not trust Tecumseh or his brother. He feared that Tecumseh might get guns from the English in Canada. The peace between America and England was uneasy—another war might come at any time.

The Wabash Valley was not part of United States territory. It belonged to the Indians. But many settlers wanted to take over the land there.

In 1809, while Tecumseh was away, Governor Harrison called a great council at Fort Wayne, Indiana. Hungry and poor, many old Chiefs went to the fort. When the council was done, Harrison had tricked the Chiefs into signing away three million acres of land for very little money!

When Tecumseh returned and heard of the
treaty, he was angry. He demanded to speak to
Governor Harrison. A council was arranged at
Vincennes, the capital of the Indiana Territory.
Tecumseh came with three hundred warriors in
eighty canoes.

At Vincennes, Tecumseh refused to go inside to
talk. He insisted that the meeting be held under
the sky of the Great Spirit. He would sit only in a
council circle so that all could hear his words.

His eyes flashed with anger as he spoke. He said that all the treaties were worthless pieces of paper. The land belonged only to the Great Spirit, who had given it to all Indians.

"Sell a country! Why not sell the air, the clouds, and the great sea, as well as the earth? Did not the Great Spirit make them all for the use of his children?"

Then Tecumseh warned Governor Harrison that his people would die before giving up their land and their way of life!

When the meeting was over, both Tecumseh and Harrison knew there would be bloodshed. In spite of the talk of peace, both men had war in their hearts.

Tecumseh hoped there was still time to find help for his people.

He traveled southward. He sent messengers and visited among the southern tribes. His message was the same wherever he spoke. *Indians must stand together or they would all fall!*

But even as Tecumseh had ridden away from the council, Harrison was giving orders to his men. *Find any excuse to destroy the village of Tecumseh and the Shawnee Prophet!*

Late in 1811, Governor Harrison led one thousand men out of Vincennes toward Tippecanoe. Infantry soldiers marched in brass-buttoned blue uniforms. Red, white, and blue feathers fluttered on their stovepipe hats.

Tecumseh had told Tenskwatawa not to make war on the Americans while he was away. But now, the Shawnee Prophet spoke strong words to his people:

"We must defend our town. My magic will protect you. The Bluecoats' gunpowder will turn to sand, and their bullets will change into raindrops. No harm will come to the warrior who fights with the Prophet!"

Just before dawn on November 6, 1811, one
hundred warriors stole into Harrison's camp.
When he heard the first war cry, the governor
mounted his horse and took charge of the battle.

Many braves fell that day. But the Prophet
was not hurt. He stayed far from the battle—
casting his spells and sending more men to die!

26

When Tecumseh returned, his dream of a nation had turned to ashes and smoke at Tippecanoe.

His hopes to unite his people had failed. Now the tribes were scattered with the wind.

Still, Tecumseh would not accept defeat. One hope remained. There was growing talk of war between England and America. If many Indians fought on the side of the British, Indian lands might be saved after all!

When the War of 1812 began, Tecumseh led braves from thirty-two tribes into Canada. Now the English made him a general.

With his warriors, Tecumseh pledged to help the English drive the Bluecoats and American settlers from Indian land.

28

The Indians made many successful raids on settlers in the northern Ohio Valley.

Then, with English soldiers, they decided to try to capture Fort Detroit from the Americans.

Tecumseh knew his side was greatly outnumbered. But he had a plan. Fearlessly, he and his warriors encircled the fort. In the dark woods, the braves called to each other with the shrill cries of coyotes and wild turkey hoots. Inside the fort, terror grew.

At dawn, Tecumseh did not attack. Instead, he paraded his men three times in and out of the woods. Their war whoops and swift movements made the Americans think there were thousands of Indians outside the fort.

Before long, a white flag flew over the fort. Tecumseh's clever trick had brought a great victory!

Tecumseh won more and more battles. As news of his victories spread, more Indians joined him.

There was no doubt that Tecumseh was helping the British win the war in the Northwest Territory.

In the winter of 1812, the Americans had a new
leader. He was the same man who had destroyed
Tecumseh's dream at Tippecanoe. William
Henry Harrison, eager for the taste of another
victory, now led an army of frontiersmen.

In February of 1813, General Harrison built a
small fort on the banks of the Maumee River in
Ohio. From there, he made plans to take Fort
Detroit back from the English. The Americans
had not liked losing this fort.

Tecumseh was eager to stop his old enemy. But he had been joined by the English General Proctor, and Proctor did not like to move quickly. It took two months to convince the British commander to attack General Harrison's forces.

Tecumseh was ready. With eight hundred warriors, he encircled Harrison's fort. But General Harrison would not fight yet. He knew that more troops were on the way.

When Tecumseh saw the flag of the American reinforcements appear in the distance, he quickly led his warriors across the river and surrounded the new troops.

General Proctor was less eager to do battle; he fired from across the river.

Both sides fought bravely, but when the battle was over, the Indians had won another victory for the English.

Now Tecumseh wanted to go back to Harrison's fort and force the general to surrender. But Proctor, still preferring the safest course of action, insisted on moving northward. He ordered the British and Indian troops to march to Fort Malden, close to the shores of Lake Erie. Here many English soldiers kept watch over the Canadian border.

Tecumseh knew that delaying an attack would give the Americans the time they needed to build their strength. Again and again, he urged General Proctor to go back and do battle. But the general did not listen.

When they arrived at Fort Malden, many warriors grew impatient. More and more of them began to drift away from the campfires.

Meanwhile, Commodore Oliver Perry was keeping his men busy building a fleet of boats. The Americans wanted to take Lake Erie from the English Navy. If they could do this, they knew the might of the English would be broken.

Finally, on September 10, 1813, a great naval battle took place on Lake Erie.

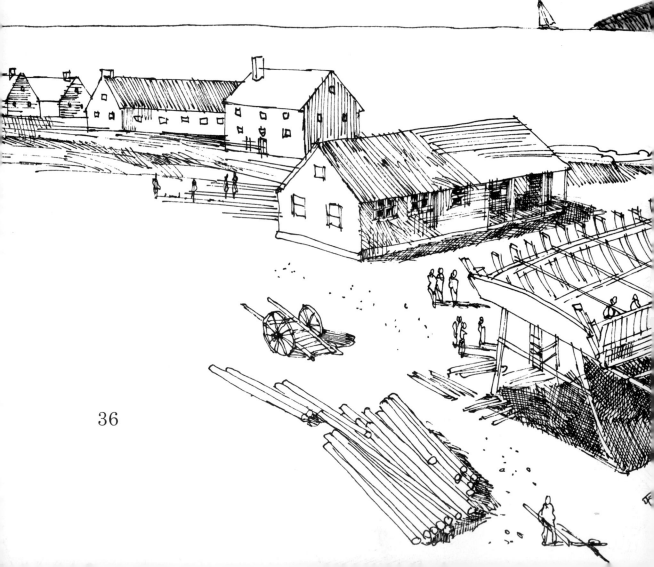

36

That day, Tecumseh and his men paddled out onto the lake. They could not see the battle, but they heard the thunder of cannons across the water.

After a fierce battle, the English fleet was destroyed. Commodore Perry had won! He sent a message to General Harrison, saying:

"We have met the enemy and they are ours!"

Now the British would finally be forced to retreat into Canada.

When Tecumseh learned of the English defeat, he knew that his great dream was finished. He brought his army of a thousand warriors to the parade ground at Fort Malden. There he spoke courageous words:

"Our lives are in the hands of the Great Spirit. We will defend our lands . . . we will never give them up!"

General Harrison lost no time. He and his soldiers moved quickly toward Fort Malden. Proctor gave the order to burn the fort, and left for Canada.

Tecumseh stared from a distance at the blazing fort, remembering the dreams of victory he had shared with his men. Now—as in his boyhood and at Tippecanoe—his dreams were turning to ashes and smoke.

There was nothing left now but shame and sorrow. Proctor had fled, leaving Tecumseh's warriors and their families to follow. The Indians were caught between two armies . . . one fleeing, one chasing.

Proctor might save his own life, but Tecumseh had no thoughts of leaving women and children to find their own way.

Slowly, the cold and hungry group of Indians followed the retreating British soldiers up the Thames River.

Harrison's army moved closer and closer. Tecumseh sent message after message begging Proctor to make a stand.

Finally, Tecumseh would go no farther. He told Proctor he would fight with or without him.

He took off his British uniform and once again put on the buckskins and war paint of a Shawnee War Chief.

On October 5, 1813, the bugle call sounded. The battle had begun.

Swiftly, the soldiers charged in two waves.

Tecumseh and his warriors stood firm. His war cry rang out through the woods.

The battle went on. When the gunpowder was spent, Tecumseh and his warriors fought with their tomahawks and knives, as in the old days.

Hand to hand in battle, Tecumseh's men fought along with their mighty Chief!

In the fading light of that terrible day, Tecumseh fell. His war cry was heard no more.

With his death, the spirit of his men also died. They carried their Chief silently into the shadows of the forest.

47

Tecumseh's dream to unite all Indians in one mighty nation is a true story of great courage. But when he died, his dream died with him. In the years to come, Tecumseh's people were pushed toward the land of the setting sun.

The Indian way of life was lost forever.